Meet the SAN FRANCISCO GIANTS

PERCY LEED

Lerner Publications ◆ Minneapolis

Stats in this book are accurate through the 2024 Major League Baseball season.

Lerner Publications Company
An imprint of Lerner Publishing Group, Inc.
241 First Avenue North
Minneapolis, MN 55401 USA

For reading levels and more information, look up this title at www.lernerbooks.com.

Main body text set in ITC Avant Garde Gothic Std.
Typeface provided by Adobe Systems.

Editor: Elena Mai **Photo Editor:** Evan Villas

Library of Congress Cataloging-in-Publication Data

Names: Leed, Percy, 1968- author
Title: Meet the San Francisco Giants / Percy Leed.
Description: Minneapolis, MN : Lerner Publications, [2026] | Series: Terrific teams (Lerner sports rookie) | Includes bibliographical references and index. | Audience: Ages 5–8 | Audience: Grades 2–3 | Summary: "The San Francisco Giants hold the record for the most wins of all time in MLB history. Explore the greatest moments, best players, and more from one of the most successful teams in the MLB"— Provided by publisher.
Identifiers: LCCN 2025015091 (print) | LCCN 2025015092 (ebook) | ISBN 9798765689691 library binding | ISBN 9798348029456 paperback | ISBN 9798765699423 epub
Subjects: LCSH: San Francisco Giants (Baseball team)—History—Juvenile literature | Baseball players—United States—Juvenile literature
Classification: LCC GV875.S34 L44 2026 (print) | LCC GV875.S34 (ebook) | DDC 796.357/640979461—dc23/eng/20250509

LC record available at https://lccn.loc.gov/2025015091
LC ebook record available at https://lccn.loc.gov/2025015092

Manufactured in the United States of America
1-1012410-54837-8/11/2025

Photo Acknowledgments
Image credits: Ed Zurga/Getty Images, p. 5; Jamie Squire/Getty Images, pp. 7, 20, 22; General Photographic Agency/Getty Images, p. 9; Elsa/Getty Images, p. 11; Bettmann/Getty Images, p. 13; Garrett W. Ellwood/Getty Images, p. 15; Bailey Hillesheim/Icon Sportswire via AP Images, p. 17; Darren Yamashita/MLB Photos via Getty Images, p. 18; Bob Kupbens/Icon Sportswire via Getty Images, p. 21; Stephen Lam/San Francisco Chronicle via Getty Images, p. 23. Design elements: Kwangmoozaa/Getty Images; Andrii Shelenkov/Getty Images; jasonclardy/Getty Images.
Cover: Trinity Machan/Icon Sportswire via AP Photo.

Table of Contents

★ CHAPTER 1 ★

Giants in the League

In September 2024, Matt Chapman batted for the San Francisco Giants. Home run!

Chapman hit two home runs in the game. The Giants beat the Kansas City Royals 9–0.

Since 1883, the Giants have won 11,541 games.

They hold the MLB record for the most wins of all time.

★ CHAPTER 2 ★

Big Moments

The Giants began in New York City. In 1905, the Giants won their first World Series. They beat the Philadelphia Athletics 4–1.

Between 1911 and 1954, the Giants won the World Series four times.

In 1958, the Giants moved to San Francisco, California.

In the 2010 World Series, the Giants beat the Texas Rangers in five games. It was their first World Series win since moving to San Francisco.

★ CHAPTER 3 ★

Best Players

Giants history is full of great players. Willie Mays played with the Giants for 21 seasons.

Mays is the only Giants player with more than 3,000 hits.

Some fans think Barry Bonds was MLB's best player. His 762 home runs are the most in MLB history.

Buster Posey was one of the best catchers in MLB. He helped the Giants win three World Series.

Each year, the Giants give the Willie Mac Award to the team's best leader.

Matt Chapman won the 2024 Willie Mac Award. He led the Giants with 27 home runs.

In 2025, Willy Adames joined the Giants. He is a star at bat and in the field.

★ CHAPTER 4 ★

Let's Go, Giants!

When the Giants won the 2010 World Series, they were just getting started.

The team also won the World Series in 2012 and 2014. The Giants have won eight total World Series.

Fans love to watch the Giants at Oracle Park.

When will the Giants win their next World Series? Fans can't wait to find out.

SAN FRANCISCO GIANTS TEAM LEADERS

Batting average:	Bill Terry, .341
Hits:	Willie Mays, 3,187
Home runs:	Willie Mays, 646
Wins:	Christy Mathewson, 372
Strikeouts:	Christy Mathewson, 2,504

Glossary

home run: a hit that allows the batter to run around all the bases and score

MLB: Major League Baseball

World Series: MLB's championship series

Learn More

Leed, Percy. *Baseball Superstars*. Lerner Publications, 2025.

Leed, Percy. *Baseball's World Series*. Lerner Publications, 2025.

Wynter, Anne. *Willie Mays: A Little Golden Book Biography*. Golden Books, 2025.

Index